Pushing

Written by Margaret MacDonald

Picture Dictionary

bike

merry-go-round

Read the picture dictionary. You will find these words in the book.

scooter

seesaw

swing

Force makes things go.
Force pushes things
to make them move.
Force makes things
go fast or slow.

What makes this bike go?
A pushing force
makes the bike go.
The rider uses his legs
to push the bike pedals.

Look at the seesaw.
Force makes the seesaw
go up and down.
When one person
pushes up, the other person
goes down.

What makes
a merry-go-round go?
Force makes
a merry-go-round go.
People push
the merry-go-round
to make it spin.

Look at this scooter.
Force makes the scooter
go fast or slow.
The boy uses his leg
to push the scooter along.

What makes this swing go? Force makes the swing go backward and forward. The swinger uses her legs to push the swing higher.

Activity Page

Make a list of things in your house and school that use a pushing force.

Do you know the dictionary words?